MEMORIES TILL MY LAST BREATHE

PREETHI SHANKAR

Contents

Prologue

Life, four letter word, which makes you learn everything helps to go through bad and good situations which sometimes makes you weak and sometimes strengthen you.

Life gives you many ups and down, low and high. But, always remember everything that happens will definitely has a reason. Just remember this and go with the flow. May be it's hard sometimes, but never give up on it so easily, it will bring good days. "GOOD THINGS TAKE TIME TO HAPPEN".

'YESTERDAY WAS HISTORY
TODAY IS A MYSTERY
TOMORROW IS A GIFT'

Everyday is special, try to make it a memory filled with happiness, spend time with family, cousin's, friends. Try to make pocket full of memories because memories are the only things that come with us till our last [end of our life].

Never judge a person on their imperfections, no one are perfect on this world everyone has imperfections. Help everyone even our enemies, achieve your dreams, live your life to the full extent, never hurt others. Whenever life hits you hard, don't get tensed just smile and let it go. Always make sure that you have a beautiful smile on your face. Don't turn life into thorns, try to make it as beautiful as your heart.

Acknowledgements

FINALLY, I thank each and every person in this novel, who helped me in this journey, thank you for teaching me so many things. Though some memories were hard which made me cry, which made my heart into broken pieces. Some memories were wonderful which made me laugh out loud which brought smile on my face. Thank you guys, thank you for filling my pocket with wonderful memories. Last but not least I would like to thank my love, my hero, my everything 'DAD'. Thank you for everything dad, thank you god for choosing me as his daughter. My cousins, relatives, friends, colleagues, my well wishers thank you so much.

CHAPTER ONE

CHAPTER 1

'EVERYONE ON THIS EARTH HAS TO OVERCOME DIFFICULTIES'.

I always heard that last born girls in the family are Dad's little princess. And, I think this is absolutely true...........

Story of PREETHI SHANKAR

Dad a person who is everything to us, an emotion, super hero, a man who is not less than God. Who sacrifices everything for family. Never expects anything in return.

1999:

1999, July 31st, Saturday at 9:00 PM Gagan mahal, Block B, Adorable girl with cute smile, beautiful face. Holding me in his hands and kissed my forehead was named as 'PREETHI'.

PREETHI- LOVE [Preethi represents love]

I was born in Hyderabad, fair, cute little face, straight and short hair, height 5.6, thin, music lover, pessimistic person, basket ball player, over thinker, love to spend time with cousins. Especially dad's little princess.

Everyone say that I look exactly like my mom. 'MOTHER AN EMOTION'.

Though I was so close to my dad, whenever I look my mom in trouble my heart gets worried. She is so beautiful from inside and outside, gorgeous, wonderful, dazzling eyes, intelligent, problem solver, supportive...etc., it will definitely take so many pages to describe about her. Sometimes we get irritated by her, but without her home is Desolate and Weird. She is such a beautiful person and wonderful.

Basically, I come from a Joint family, with 10 cousin's who were just annoying, silly, sometimes frustrating, may be sisters are born to irritate us. 'A family which stays together, eats together, spends time to together is always a happy family. Enjoying very moment with cousin's, playing, cracking jokes on each other, laughing when one falls down, fighting for silly things, still we were close by hearts.

And, our names which goes like this.....

Pranaya [Pranu]: elder sister and responsible

Pranitha [Sony]: the Angry girl

Rajeshwari [Gundu]: workaholic and skinny

Pragathi [Preethi]: that's me you will come to know about me at by the end of this novel

Hemavathi [Chinni]: Tv lover [covers every channel on tv]

Lavanya [Sweety]: Book worm, Brahmanandam [laughs on each and every thing]

Chaitanya [Chaiti]: over strict, rules minder

Sravani [Kashi]: Dad of violence, not less than Angrybird

Poojitha [Pooji]: Doctor and chef of our family

Sai charan [Sai]: the one only boy in our family, 1 brother for 9 sisters, most loved and food lover.

You can just imagine how weird things we have done....

We did our schooling in Holy Mary High School for girls. Our elder sister the responsible one use to hold our hands and we use to go by walk to school it looked exactly like Goose train. Running through shops to buy candies, irritating her, sharing Guava, pulling each other bags. It was very fun those moments were really wonderful.

COUSIN'S

It's not just a word, whenever we see them a lot of memories come to our minds.

Some, instances from our childhood memory, A fine afternoon we all went for a marriage at Khaja Mansion, Masab tank. We were so hungry so we had a visit to food court and thought to have some deserts, and when we went to desert stall our eyes went to through Gulab Jamun and that smell dragged us towards it. We rushed to the counter and took 4 Gulab Jamun. Have you guys ever observed that there will be fans placed at different spots in wedding, swinging from one corner to another. As it was month of May, we sat right in front of the fan, as the fan turned towards us, cup of sweet from my cousin hand got flew away and got landed on some uncle's head. LOL

Summer:

Whenever we think about summer things that come to our mind are Mangoes, Half day schools, Ice barfi, Ice cream, Morning schools, summer holidays, papad at evening. Gathering around Ice cream bandi for ice creams and our granny use to pay for it. A perfect planning, procedure and implementation how to spend that 5rs pocket money. Everything that we do with cousin's is a great memory and wonderful.

There were so many weird things that we did, but that's common in every family. We still laugh on the things we did at our childhood.

Especially Sundays, Sunday was so joyful, waking up at 4:00 AM in the morning, watching Oswald, Noddy, Thomas and train, Tom and jerry.

Enter Caption

"IF YOU MISS THOSE DAYS, JUST GO BACK AND RECOLLECT ALL YOUR MEMORIES".

I WISH I COULD BE THE CHILD AGAIN
The child with a little brain
The child with a sweet heart
The child with a innocent face
The child with a great love
--LAVANYA

Then, here comes the great Adventure

CHAPTER TWO

CHAPTER 2

At last, entered into danger zone, we can find only books in this danger zone nothing else. In the year 2013-2014 I did my 10th class. Basically, it's just 10th class like all other classes but people make us feel like it is 3rd World war, the rules for every 10th class students, they can't attend any function, can't go to parties, no phones, no games, no chitchatting, no Television, only thing they can do is study, study, study, study like a book worm. Here comes the real war 'MATHS' oh god is the most terrified subject, a book covered with full of problems struggling hard to find solutions which never comes to my mind and not even in my notes. Mathematics is like an enemy to me.

Finally, 2014, May 18th, 11.00 AM sharp, Tuesday, 'RESULTS'. Tensed faces, news channel on every Television, then that time occurred to enter Hall ticket number, hands were shivering, heart was beating faster, then it appeared as 'SERVER BUSY', 'SERVER BUSY' thrice 'SERVER BUSY' that word was so irritating and thought to break my computer, for the 4th time I received my results. I was so happy and little bit shocked that I secured more than I expected. I was so so so happy because I secured more than my sister.

My sister started crying after looking at my marks, but seeing her cry made me so happy [hahaahaha]. This time mathematics was my friend, thank you mathematics. My dad always had confidence on me that I will secure good marks. His blessings were always with me, and his support. On my first exam he dropped at my exam center and waited over there till 12.30, he made me wake up at early in the mornings. He came near me and told

'BABY, I KNOW YOU WILL DO THIS, AND MAKE ME PROUD, ALWAYS BE HAPPY AND SHINING.

Those words gave me courage and build up my confidence.

2014:

First day of my college, 'COLLEGE' which makes us feel that we are no more kids now, new dresses, new books, new friends, new culture everything was new. St. Ann's junior college for Girls, CEC [Commerce, Economics, Civics], college taught me many things.

First day, Wednesday, June 12th, 8.30 PM, entered the classroom and sat beside a girl. Whenever I look at her 1 thing that comes to my mind is 'PANDA'. She looked exactly like panda. Short, Dusky col0ur, Long and straight hair, innocent face, beautiful by heart, zero hatred exactly opposite to me. Never thought she would become so important in my life. This continued in my degree also, I thought at least now I'll get rid of her[hahaha], but she joined me in degree also. 'NIKITHA' [best friend].

DEGREE:

2017, Friday, 8.30 AM, Villa Marie degree college for women, unexpectedly everything in my life like school, inter and degree was done at girl's school and women college. I have never been to coeducation. Villa Marie was posh college, good ambience, cultural events, campus placements, seminars, labs, life became so busy, and our friendship became so strong. We were so close that we maintained same attendance percentage 75.1 exactly same, our friends use to bet on us, my friends use to ask me whether I coming to college or not, and if in case I say 'No, I'm not coming' they get fixed that she is also not going to come.

One fine day, we use to have Tally class in our computer lab, we were sharing computers, our lecturer was dictating notes and whole class was noting down it, class was so silent and we both were fighting for the place, she never allow me to put my book on the table, in between of that fight we pushed keyboard and it fell down and everyone were looking at us, even the letter 'p' was broken, we were looking at each other and her idiotic expression made me laugh so badly that my lecturer told us to stand outside till the bell rings. Whenever I look at keyboard my mind goes through this incident.

The way she look, her expressions, her innocence, helpful nature, sometimes numb, fatty fellow my cute Panda. She says that she is a great cook but the way she explained about chicken curry in placements is unforgettable. I don't think you are a chef, and especially your Tomato curry and that tomato saucc which you put in Tomato curry is so disgusting, please don't try that receipe when you get married.

Enter Caption

She was always supportive, she never left me alone, she know everything about me, my weakness and strength. Laughing at serious things, teasing everyone, sharing lunch box, fighting for seats, those days were really great.

Debhora [dabba] thank you so much dabba you were always supportive and helped me in every situation, the time you spend for me, though you are busy, at church, sleeping, busy with family, you never ignored me you were always with me. Exactly like a boyfriend [hahahahaha]. I don't need any boyfriend if you are with me. 'I LOVE YOU DABBA'.

Pravalika, every gang has a short friend, my gang has too, pravalika [potti].over excited, lipstick lover, selfie queen, late comer. She is the one who is pissed off between me and nikitha. We use to tease her a lot, thank you for bearing all our nuisance. Thank you for that tasty food by aunty. Do, you remember the day when you made biryani for us, oh god, it was so tasty, but we know that it was not made by you, that credit goes to nikitha. Please stop irritating me atleast now. We both had lots of memories.

Nikitha do, you still remember our accounts exam, we did not even had a proper notes, but our exam went awesome, though we were far but our combine studies went awesome.

Friends teach us so many things, we can share everything with them, though I was 19 years old I was so dumb and my friends explained me everything and we call it as 'BIOLOGY', this class was really fun. Nick names which give to our friends, Debhora [dabba], Archana, Purna [alien], Satvika, Durga [darga], Harshitha [amul baby].

We feel happy that we are in college and no more kids now, but sometimes we feel to go back to that school because we can't celebrate children's day, teacher's day, we don't show any interest to visit college for independence day and many other things.

February 2nd, Somajiguda, Jaya gardens, we had an college event Commercio esscena, and I was in dance, bunking classes to practice dance, before the event we got our costume and when I looked at our costume I was literally shocked, skirt was till my knees, pink and black color, it was so weird and comedy and I went to try it, and when I came out the way you both [nikitha, archana] laughed at me, I know I looked exactly like village girl. I DON'T WHY THIS HAPPENS TO ME VERY FREQUENTLY

CHAPTER THREE

CHAPTER 3

I DON'T KNOW WHY THIS HAPPENS TO ME VERY FREQUENTLY

Our exams were about to start, combined studies, spending our pocket money on xerox, assignments, night outs, early morning studies, alarm. All of sudden, my heart started beating slow, eyes were closing, mind got numb, unable to breath, may be that's due to tension, dad took me for a ride on his activa, 5:00 AM searching for a peaceful place, which gives relaxation to my mind and heart. Then we went to necklace road, sat on a bench, dad brought a cup of tea and he told me one thing

"Preethi always believe in yourself and listen to your heart. I'm always with you and I know that my little princess is not less than anyone". Those word brought tears in my eyes and when I looked at his face my confidence level was boosted. My heart started beeping normally, as expected my exams were Awesome.

I always had an intention that 'WE BECOME BLACK IF WE DRINK TEA'. But from that day tea became an emotion.

'ANY TEA/COFFEE LOVERS', LET'S TAKE A TEA BREAK.

I WISH I COULD BE THE TEEN AGAIN

The teen who didn't care how people looked at her
The teen who didn't care what others thought of her
The teen who didn't care how people treated her
The teen who didn't care what others did to her

CHAPTER 4

'Everyone comes in your life for a reason, either to be yours forever or to leave you with a lesson that lasts you with forever'.

'LIFE HAS BECOME LIKE A RAINBOW AFTER MEETING YOU'

2018:

DASARA, the festival of Telangana, Dussera is celebrated for 9 days called as Navratri, the most beautiful and joyful festival. People play 'Bathukamma' and it is celebrated a day before Dasara.

Friday, 7:00 PM, Day 7, colourful lights, fragrance of roses, kids playing, smell of tasty food, temple filled with people and Diya's, looking around all of sudden my eyes went through a hand which had 'Glucose'.

Glucose the thing which makes me terrified, I still remember that day, White kurta, blue jeans, Colourful cloth round your neck, a red thread on your right hand, glucose on your left hand, innocent face, short hair, trimmed beard, bright eyes, cute smile on your face, tall, fair, thin, King by heart---RAHUL

I never thought you would become so close to me. Moments spend with you were excellent and I would never forget them.

When I saw glucose on his hand I was little bit terrified and thought to talk with him regarding that, so I texted him in Instagram and it started through Instagram it went so long and we started our conversation almost in every app Messenger, Snapchat, Hike, Whatsapp, Instagram, Truecaller etc., almost every app.

I don't know whether this is attraction or love. We became so close and started sharing things with each other.

Finally, our first meet 2019, October 20th, Donut house, it was little weird and shy but it went Awesome. After that first meeting we came to know more about each other, Late night conversations, Long hour calls, blush on faces, praying for each other, gossips, possessiveness, jealous, meetings etc.,

2020, May 24th, Saturday and I still remember that day the day when you said 'I LOVE YOU'. Function at home, Mom and Dad 25th anniversary, relatives, pending works, even though we had 2hrs conversation and the way you said it. We met in the year 2018 and you said it in the year 2020....... Isn't that weird. Even it's weird, those words made me smile and butterflies in my stomach I was unable to give you a reply back.

Whenever we meet, you use to book an uber auto for me. Following me, waiting till I get into auto, those things really made me happy, caring, love....

You never made an excuse, when I asked you to meet me may it be your office hours, lunch break, even when you are with your friends, nap time, Sunday or family time. You always made time for me though we fight a lot. We are not less than Tom and Jerry. The way you make me laugh.

Whenever I talk with you, I just feel stress free, happy and spark in my eyes.

I still remember that HUG, I forgot everything and just felt that warm in your hug,

September 28th
Clock ticking 5:00 PM,
A blissful evening,
Romantic weather,
An Introvert girl, but his presence made her extrovert,
Finally, two souls met for the first time
Feeling secured in his Arms
Wrapped each other
But, deep down her heart dropped tears
And, there was something special in that 'FIRST HUG'

Enter Caption

CHAPTER FIVE

CHAPTER 5

I always feel insecured with boys may be because I was never into coeducation before. But, I never felt insecured with you.

The way I spoiled you drink night, Jubliee hills, 10:30 PM and I asked you to meet me, you thought it was just a meet, no it was not to meet it was plan to drop me at home but you had plan with your friend's, wines shops were about to close and the way you asked me to go by auto 'Please maa go by auto, wines shops will be closed'. I didn't even try to understand you, I know I was little stubborn at that moment, and made sure that you drop me home safely exactly at door. Your frustrated face, I still remember your pleasing expressions, that angry face. Finally, he dropped at home and the bad thing that happened after dropping at home was that your bike was caught by traffic police and your bike was at police station till next day. When you explained about this the next morning I laughed so badly and you did not even scold me for that.

Those all moments were the best part of my life. As we know people do change according to time no one remains the same. So, with you

FROM

Late night conversations to no conversations

No more calls
No more tom and jerry
No more wishes on

Once, it was time where you made sure to meet at any cost, but now you are not even bothered to see my text or lift my calls. My messages make you irritated, my calls make you angry. You never made an attempt to call back even after seeing my missed calls, even though I was waiting with a hope that you will call me.

Those days were really so hard, maybe I had over expectations, I know it's not your fault. We had a huge fight that day, I know I was little rude but situation made me, I thought you will understand me there was a long gap between us. After a month when I tried calling you, you told me one thing

'PLEASE DON'T TEXT OR CALL ME, I HAVE MOVED ON AND I HAVE A GIRLFRIEND'.

Those words made me cry, but I never told you because maybe you found I girl better than me and I want you to be happy. Maybe she loves you more than I do. I tried my best to be away from you. There is a saying that 'FIRST LOVE NEVER DIE'S'. May be this is absolutely correct.

Does feelings change so easily, how can a person forget their loved one so easily. Maybe you never loved me. Whenever I visit our spot, it makes me cry. It makes me remember the day which I never want to recollect the worst memory of my life...........

CHAPTER SIX

CHAPTER 6

The memory which I hate the most and never want to go back to it, I don't know whether you remember it or not. The most painful and worst part of our journey. The day when you left me on road, knowing that I don't even have data to book a auto because you always use to book for me, alone on that road and I was waiting there for more than 2hrs, for the first time in this 22yrs I felt I was all alone, those silent roads, empty streets were terrifying and they filled my eyes with tears which were unstoppable and you did not even tried to make a call or message to ask whether I reached home safely, one thing that bothered me a lot is, How can a person sleep peacefully after leaving their loved one's in trouble.

This situation made me realized that, yes, you have changed a lot and moved on, but why doesn't my heart accept it, why it always thinks about you, a heavy rainfall makes me thinks about you whether you are safe or not? When you don't check my message or away for more than 3 to 4hrs why my heart gets worried? Why, why, why?

It's almost been 3 and half years now, faced many up's and down's. Imagined a beautiful wedding and wonderful future with you. There were so many people who have been flirting with me but my feelings never changed for you, I always same feeling on you, though you scolded me, left me pain, angry on me. I always had same feelings on you.

That's because 'I HAVE ALWAYS SEEN MY DAD IN YOU, WHENEVER I'M WITH YOU I FEEL LIKE I'M WITH MY DAD. THAT'S THE BIGGEST THING FOR EVERY GIRL. TO GET A PERSON LIKE THEIR FATHER'.

'IF A GIRL IS IN LOVE WE CAN SEE IT IN HER SMILE, IF A BOY IS IN LOVE WE CAN SEE IT IN HIS EYES'. Maybe you never saw it in my smile, a smile which comes when I'm with you, that smile when I talk with you, that smile is no more. Sometimes my heart just wanted to hug you tightly and wanted to clear everything but never made an attempt to do that

I never thought 'LOVE IS PAIN'. Lost respect on it. This pain took me into depression and went through glucose. That situation made me weak, then I realized my dad is with me, I can't make him sad with my problems and thought to start a new life.

I know your responsibilities made you to take this decision, but thank you for those wonderful memories they will always remain with me, thank you for being supportive at times, thankyou for scolding me, thank you for being caring, thank you for making me laugh out loud at difficulities.

I love you so much, even now when I look at you I feel happy. My feelings for you will never change.

Breaking my heart into pieces
You just moved on in life and, never turned back
Is, that my mistake
To trust you blindly
Why? Does this heart never stops beating for you
Why? Do these eyes always search for you
Why? Do these tears never stop

Won’t they stop rolling down my cheeks
But, I’m always happy for you
May be the girl you find loves you more than this Heart did!

CHAPTER SEVEN

2020, December 21st, Monday 8:00 PM, the day I was about to enter into corporate field, though heart was beeping fast, my eyes with happiness that I got a 'JOB'. My first journey without dad, Uppal, NSL Arena, Sykes, crowded with new joiners, freshers and experienced. I can't even believe that I'm grown up, starting of my independent life. Everything was going good on that day.

2021:

A new year and new resolutions, done with training, time for production, night shift, late night dinner, coffee, morning logout, new friends, more responsibilities.

I was so excited about my first salary thinking that I can give to my dad, he was so happy and seeing his happy face made me so happy.

'SALARY COMES LIKE TORTOISE AND GOES LIKE RABBIT'.

As I said earlier there will be many people coming into our lives, some teach us good lessons,

A fine day, when we were at office, our team called us for meeting to discuss about deficit hours and I had 58 hours of deficit I was on the top and other was shiva he had 57 hours and we looked at each other, though we were in the same team but never seen him before.

'SHIVA', curly hair, spectacles, maroon shirt, blue jeans, white shoes, black, maintaining a good gym body, tall, brown eyes.

Day by day we became so close and our friendship turned into relationship, A beautiful relation—'BROTHER AND SISTER'

'A BROTHER FROM ANOTHER MOTHER'.

I always had a wish to have a brother like him, though brothers tease and irritate their sisters, they are so caring, possessive, supporter, responsible, thief [stealing our chocolates], sometimes pleasing, sometimes scolding, late comer and expecting us to open the door with knowing to dad. It's a beautiful relation.

After meeting this person, I never wished for brother, 'SHIVA' you were exactly a brother whom I wished to have.

Your caring nature, respect which you give to women, our night coffee, tiffin near our office, gossips, evening tea, especially the park area and the bench were we use to sit and enjoying those old songs.

The night when we were late and our logout got extended time was almost 10.30 PM and the obligation which you took, to drop me home safely and go back to Kompally. Uppal to Khairthabad and Khairthabad to Kompally. I was really happy on that day because I really felt that I got a brother and you proved it.

You were always supportive professionally and personally, especially your ringtone which makes me laugh out loud even when I'm at bad mood, angry, stressed and frustrated, please don't change it.

My care taker,

Protecting me from every difficulty,

Being supportive in every situation

People say that this is the best bond in our life. Your presence made my journey complete.

Thank you for coming into my journey and making it as beautiful as rainbow.

Though we fight a lot, but tears in your eyes make me cry. So' don't make me cry because my foundation is so expensive.

Though we are not from same womb, your presence never made me feel the emptiness of having an own brother.

.........PREETHI SHANKAR

This corporate field taught me to many things, to be independent, to overcome situations strongly, sometimes those night shifts spoiled my health still I learnt many things. We to moved to different teams and different process, meeting new team members, new team leads, everyone was so close and treated as their sister, I got so many nick names......

Thalli, Chitti, Babeamma, Madam, that was really cool and good.

Life was going so perfectly, office to home, weekends with family, outings with cousins, shopping with dad, movie plans with office friends, happy and proud to pay dad's shopping bill, well celebrated festivals with cousin's and family.

I wished that this year should bring me good days, when everything goes perfect god will test us and then a storm occurred in my life.

CHAPTER EIGHT

CHAPTER 8

A STORM OCCURRED

Early in the morning at 5:30 AM, morning walk, alone on road, streets dark as night, ear dopes plugged in.

6:00 AM, Dad's phone started ringing, phone was dropped from his hand, questions from family, dad rushed to hospital

[Stranger on the phone call] Hello, this is Rakesh, your daughter Preethi is met by an accident and got admitted in hospital.

Care hospital, Banjara hills, emergency ward, glucose injected, then dad entered into emergency ward, oxygen mask, Doctors just gave 24 hours, dad standing in front of me, his hands were shivering, eyes in his eyes. That's the last time I saw his face

Relatives, friends, families, even the people who don't like me started praying for me, tears in eyes, lots of prayers, huge rain, lost minds, heavy hearts.

ICU, every moment, every memory got recollected, those childhood memories, time spend with cousin's, my wish to get ready at my sister[pranu] wedding, to dance at her Bharath, haldi, mehendi, so many things I wished to do. I'll not be with them, I will not be in any function, marriages, no more chitchatting, laughing at each other,

I'll just be in your memories. My friends, promise which I made to nikitha to attend her wedding and to eat a lot at her wedding, but I'm so sorry nikitha that I'm breaking my promise I did not do this wantedly situation made this. Even at that last stage my heart was worried about my first love, for the last time I want to tell you that—I always love you, no matter what happens.

And, especially my dad, my super hero, he always told me that – 'I cannot live without you'. How can he live without me, that thought made me more sick and depressed.

It's almost been 2 days in ICU, missing everyone, cousin's, friends, missing my dad, our evening tea, chats with him, dance, music at every evening. Recollecting everything was most painful moment, that moment was like 'HELL'.

Finally, heart beat was going slower, machines beeping, clock ticking 5:30 PM, heavy hearts, silent rooms, eyes with full of tears, huge prayers, dad standing near the window, nurse rushing with injections and medicines, kept at ventilator, last stage, doctor's trying hard to save.

Doctor asked dad to go in and I never thought it will be last time to see him, tears were unstoppable, hands were still shivering, he cried out loud, and holding my hand he asked me to wake up, kissed my forehead as he did 22yrs back on July 31st, 1999 the day when I was born. Everything was finished, I just asked him to give me a promise that 'HE SHOULD BE ALWAYS SIMLING'. I can't see tears in his eyes. I'll be always beside you, whether it's good or bad. Heart beat was finished...............................

CHAPTER NINE

CHAPTER 9

2021:

December 10th, Saturday 6:00 AM, early mornings, Flowers blossomed, Peaceful streets, Children enjoying their cycle rides, Birds flying, Winds blowing, Dogs running behind Bikes, roads were noisy.

Dad Sitting on a bench, watching that beautiful sunrise, Grass touching his feet, remembering all those memories and I got tea for both of us, Yes, I got my life back. May be god heard his prayers and gave me my heart beat. Enjoying that hot tea in that cool weather and we had a great ride

Enter Caption

Returned home with chicken and mutton and my favorite leg piece and my cousin's waiting at home, we had great time and I was looking at all my cousin's face which I thought I would never see them again. I was so happy and everyone were happy.

LIFE :

When life turns as dark as night
When life turns as sour as bitter gourd
Life jumps as second bump
Every second is precious
Don't give up
Life is like a journey, keep on moving
We take ticket to one destination and life drops us at another destination
Don't give up when life turns your destination
Never turn it into thorns
Turn it into pocket full of roses
Don't give up
Life shows up's and down's
Accept all the downs which strengthen you and
Praising life for all the up's
Don't ever give up on it
Every moment is a miracle
Coming up with new surprises
At, the end it turns as wonderful as you create....

PREETHI SHANKAR

My Super Hero

Always remember that what ever happens in your life your dad, super hero is always with you, supporting through out the life, maybe he is angry at times, but he always thinks to give you a better and wonderful life.

'ALWAYS LOVE AND RESPECT YOUR PARENTS'.

This is the story of Preethi shankar, A story about wonderful dad, my super hero. 'I LOVE YOU DAD'.......

A 10yr old boy
Being separated from his mother
No father to support him
Carrying the family burden on his shoulder
Moving towards the 'LIFE'
A 10yr old boy
Who don't even have an idea about World,
Working in ration shop for 5 rupees
No proper clothes to wear
No footwear, walking miles and miles to save 5 rupees,
So, that he can feed his family
Family, relatives, society
No one supported him, due to some reasons.
Life gave him many difficulties
Facing all the struggle in life
Overcoming then with a smile and moved on
Finally,
Achieving the level of god
Acquiring all the super powers of god by his dedication
Leading a happy 'LIFE'
#PAPA
Maybe you are not perfect to others
But, you are my super hero

And, I'm always your little princess
Proud to be daughter of 'SHANKAR'
#PREETHI SHANKAR

Enter Caption

Printed by Libri Plureos GmbH in Hamburg, Germany